♠ *This Book Belongs To* ♠

_____

# 90 DAYS
## PRAYING WITH
## GOD

By Becky Brooks

A Journal to
Focus Your
Next 90 Days
of Prayer

90 Days Praying With God
by Becky Brooks

Published by
Cross Point Publishing
N8012 480th Street
Menomonie, Wisconsin 54751
www.crosspointpublishing.com

Cover Design by: Jason M. Brooks
Cover photo courtesy of: www.morguefile.com

Find us on Facebook at:
www.facebook.com/CrossPointPublishing

Follow us on Twitter at:
@xpointpub

Cross Point offers great prices on bulk orders of our books. Contact our sales team to learn more. sales@crosspointpublishing.com

# Check Out These Other Journal's From Becky Brooks

## 90 Days Walking With God
*A Journal to Keep Track of Your Daily Food, Exercise, Thoughts and Prayers*

### ISBN: 978-0615740812

## 90 Days Connecting With God
*A Bible Study Journal To Help You Connect On A Deeper Level With God*

**Coming Spring 2013**

✝

*Do not be anxious
about anything, but in
every situation,
by prayer and petition,
with thanksgiving,
present your
requests to God.
And the peace of God,
which transcends all
understanding,
will guard your hearts
and your minds in
Christ Jesus.*

*Philippians 4: 6-7*

✝

*I have found that writing out my prayers is a great way to stay focused while praying, and it allows me to go back and read over where I was and where God has brought me.*

*By doing this prayer journal, I hope you find yourself in some wonderfully deep prayers with our Lord, and that you too will see the Lord working in your life through your prayers.*

*Your Sister in Christ,*

*Becky Brooks*

# ♠ Day One

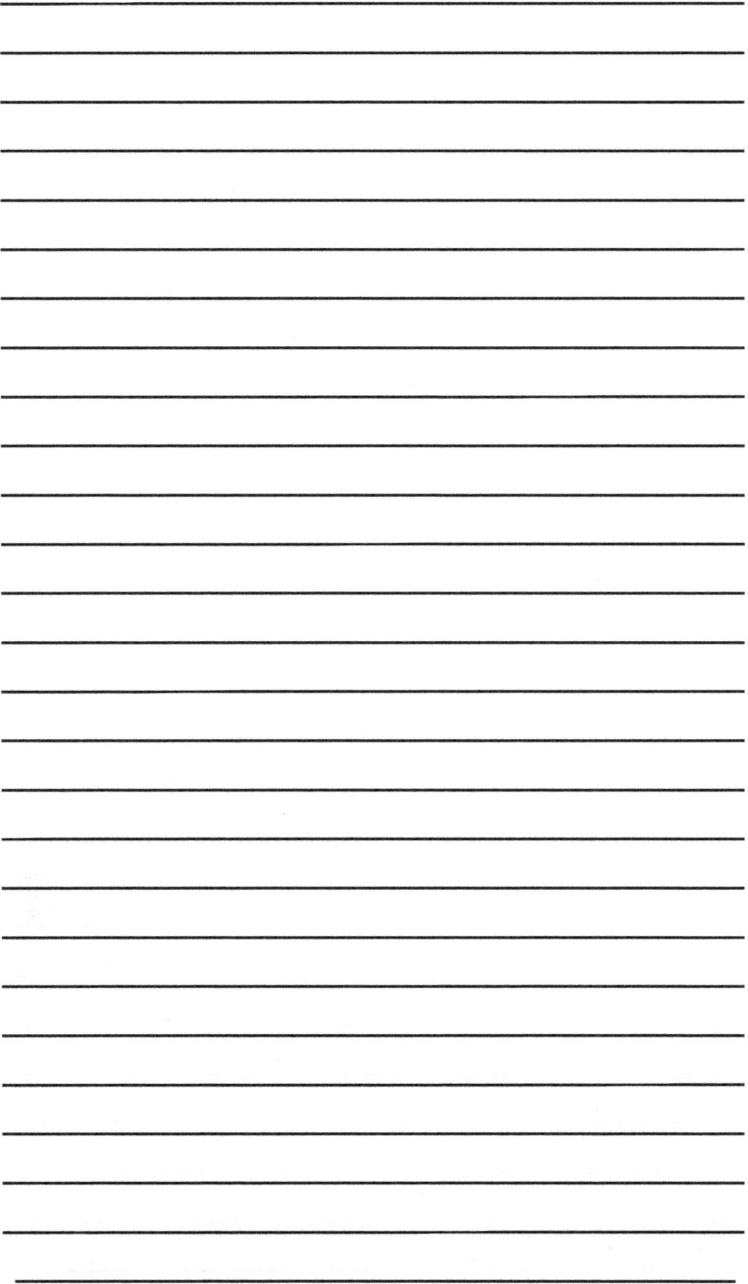

# ♠ Day Two

---
---
---
---
---
---
---
---
---
---
---
---
---
---
---
---
---
---
---
---
---
---
---
---

# ♠ Day Three

# ♠ Day Four

# ♠ Day Five

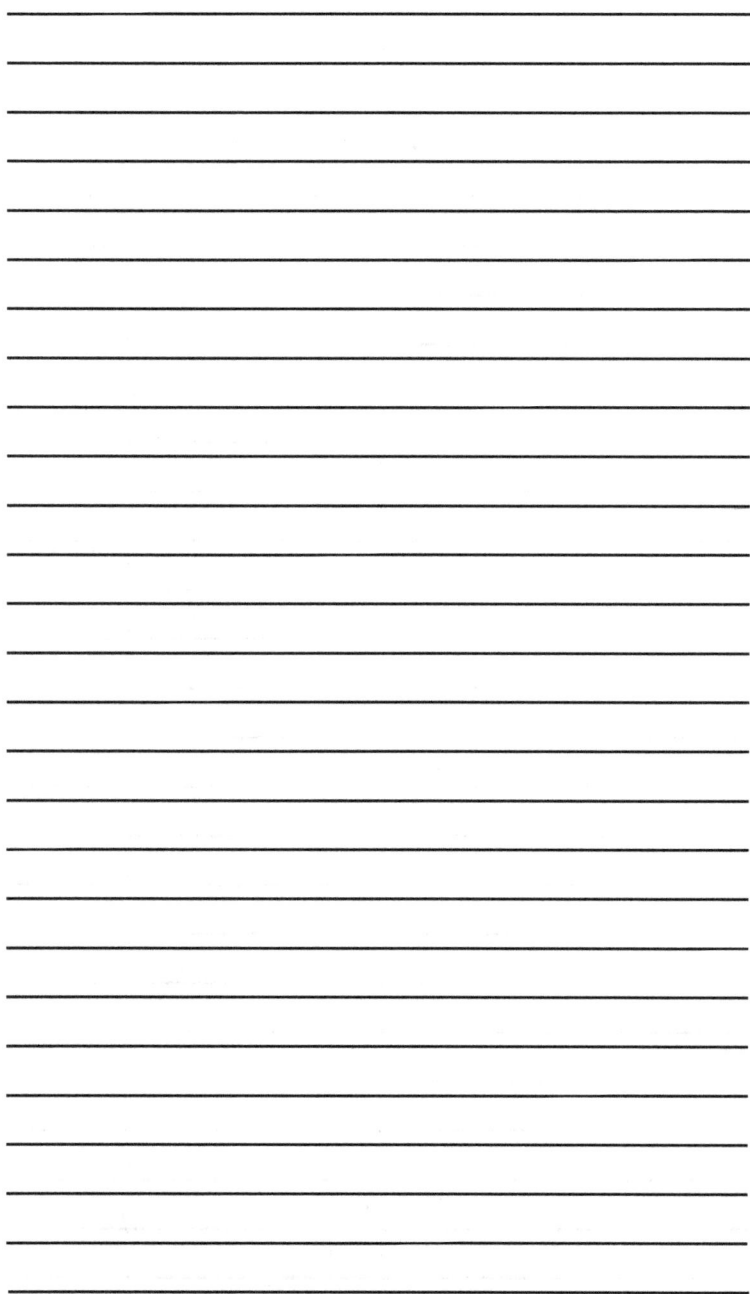

# ♠ *Day Six*

_____
_____
_____
_____
_____
_____
_____
_____
_____
_____
_____
_____
_____
_____
_____
_____
_____
_____
_____
_____
_____
_____
_____
_____
_____

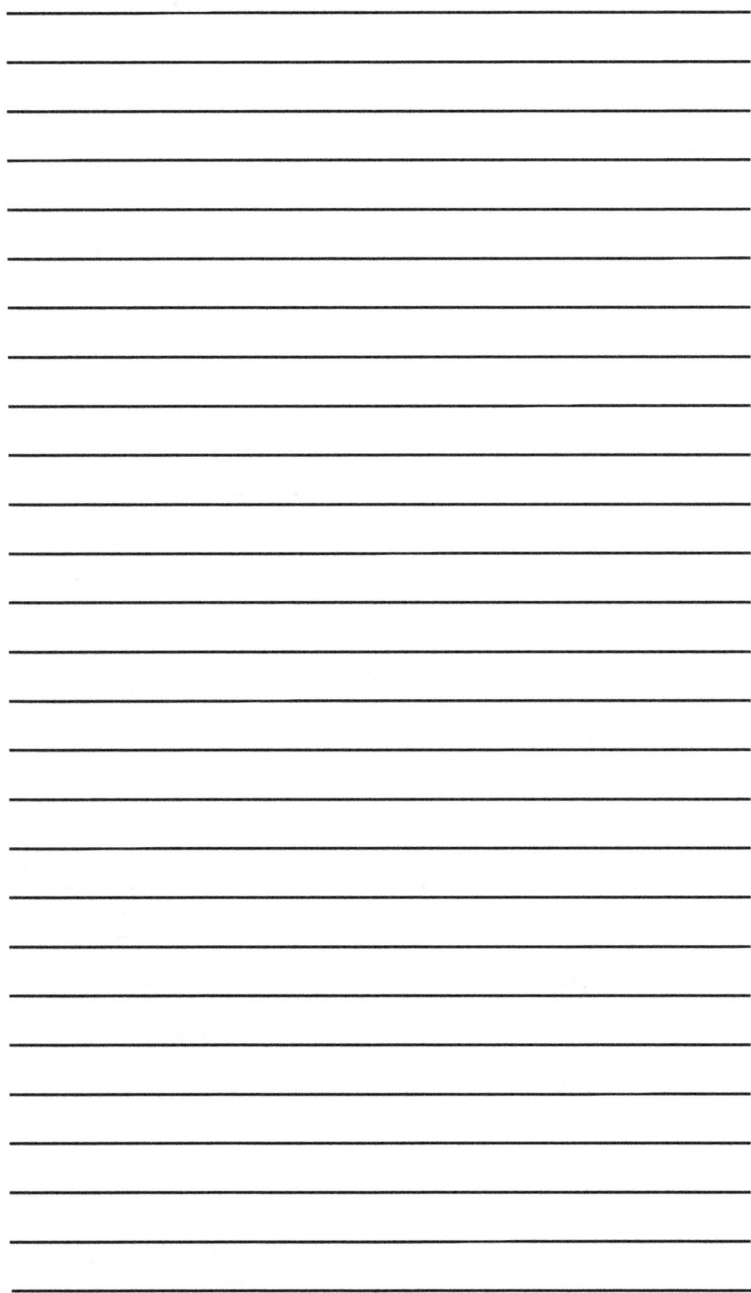

# ♠ *Day Seven*

_____

_____

_____

_____

_____

_____

_____

_____

_____

_____

_____

_____

_____

_____

_____

_____

_____

_____

_____

_____

_____

_____

_____

_____

# ♠ Day Eight

# ♠ *Day Nine*

# ♠ *Day Ten*

# ♠ *Day Eleven*

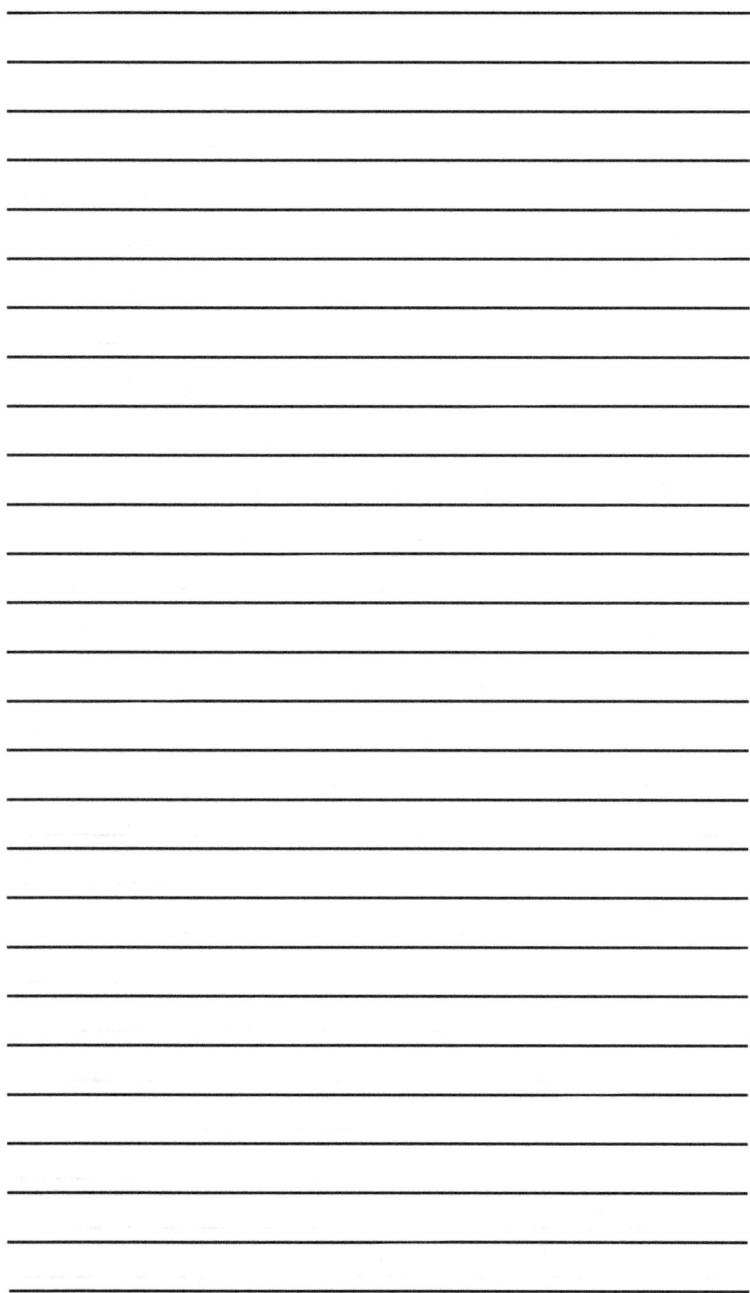

# ♠ *Day Twelve*

_____

_____

_____

_____

_____

_____

_____

_____

_____

_____

_____

_____

_____

_____

_____

_____

_____

_____

_____

_____

_____

_____

_____

# ♠ *Day Thirteen*

# ♠ *Day Fourteen*

# ♠ *Day Fifteen*

# ♠ *Day Sixteen*

# ♠ *Day Seventeen*

# ♠ Day Eighteen

# ♠ *Day Nineteen*

# ♠ Day Twenty

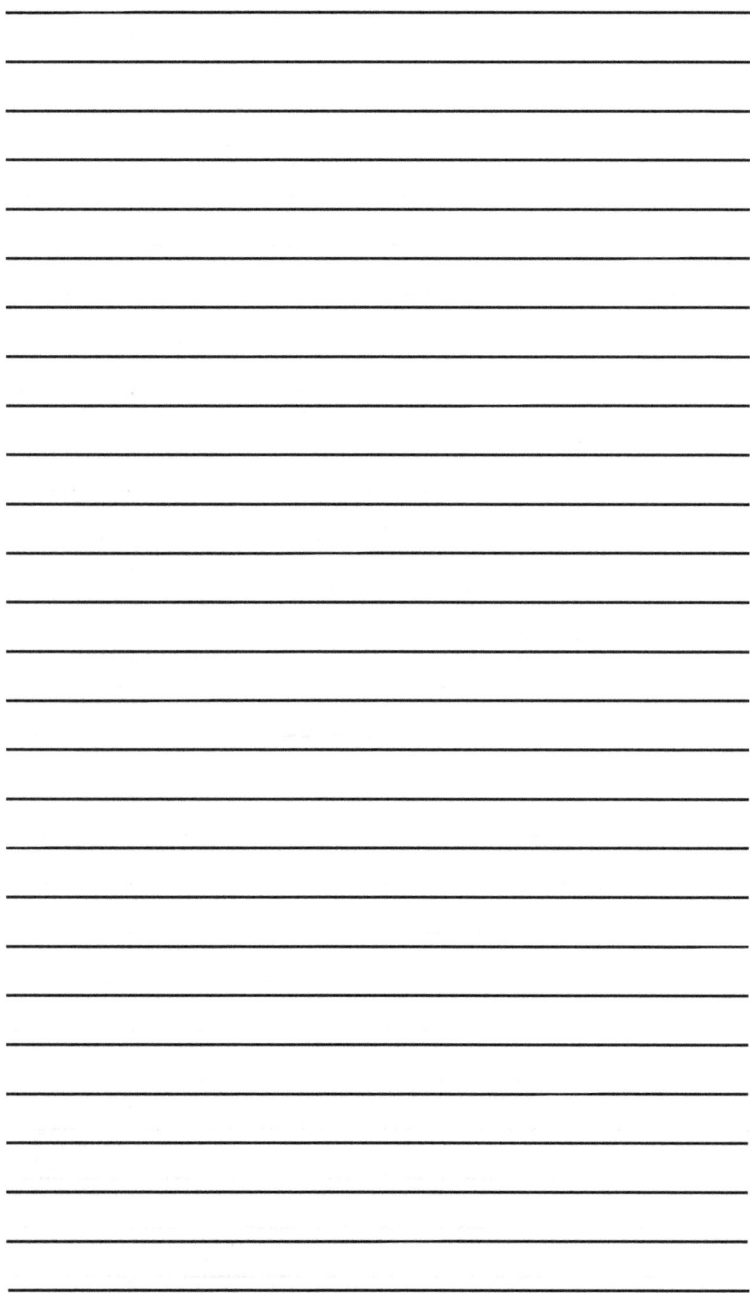

# ♠ *Day Twenty~One*

_____

_____

_____

_____

_____

_____

_____

_____

_____

_____

_____

_____

_____

_____

_____

_____

_____

_____

_____

_____

_____

_____

_____

_____

# ♠ *Day Twenty~Two*

# ♠ Day Twenty~Three

# ♠ *Day Twenty~Four*

# ♠ *Day Twenty~Five*

# ♠ *Day Twenty~Six*

# ♠ *Day Twenty~Seven*

# ♠ *Day Twenty~Eight*

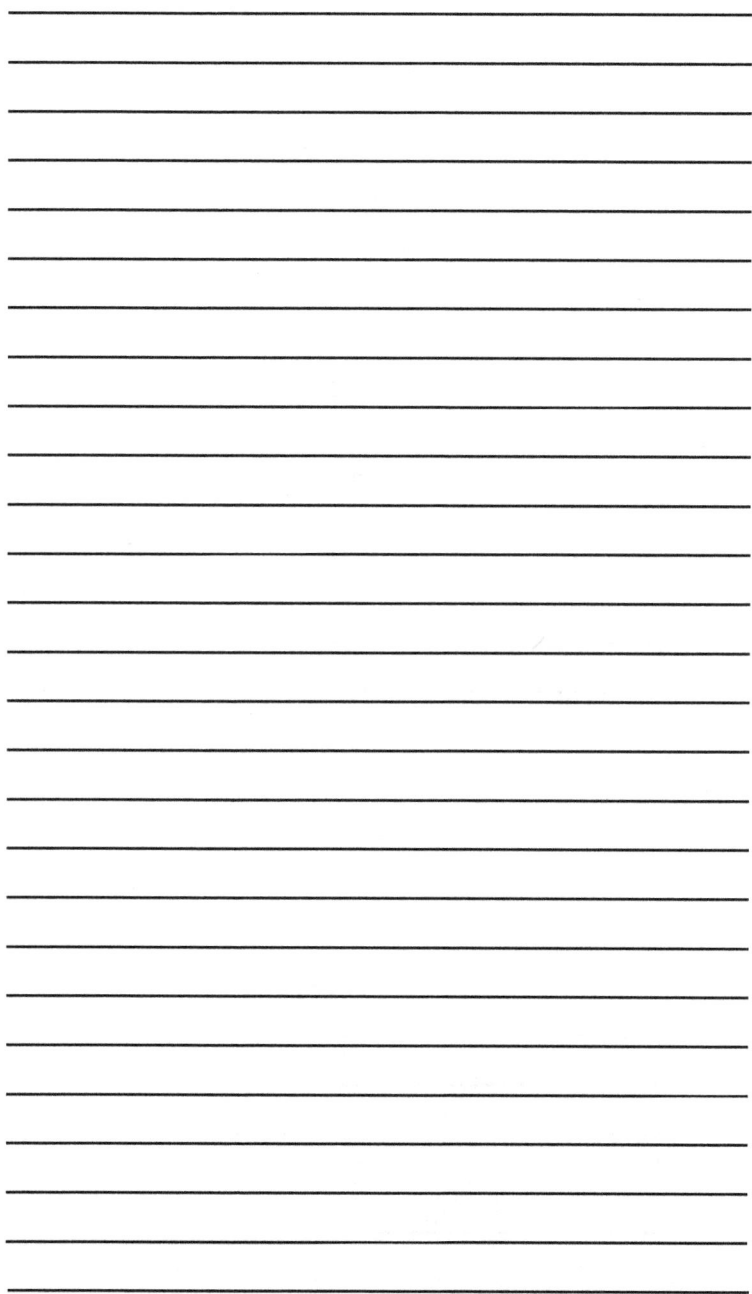

# ♠ *Day Twenty~Nine*

_____

_____

_____

_____

_____

_____

_____

_____

_____

_____

_____

_____

_____

_____

_____

_____

_____

_____

_____

_____

_____

_____

_____

# ♠ *Day Thirty*

# ♠ *Day Thirty~One*

# ♠ *Day Thirty~Two*

# ♠ *Day Thirty~Three*

# ♠ Day Thirty~Four

# ♠ Day Thirty~Five

# ♠ *Day Thirty~Six*

# ♠ *Day Thirty~Seven*

# ♠ *Day Thirty~Eight*

# ♠ *Day Thirty~Nine*

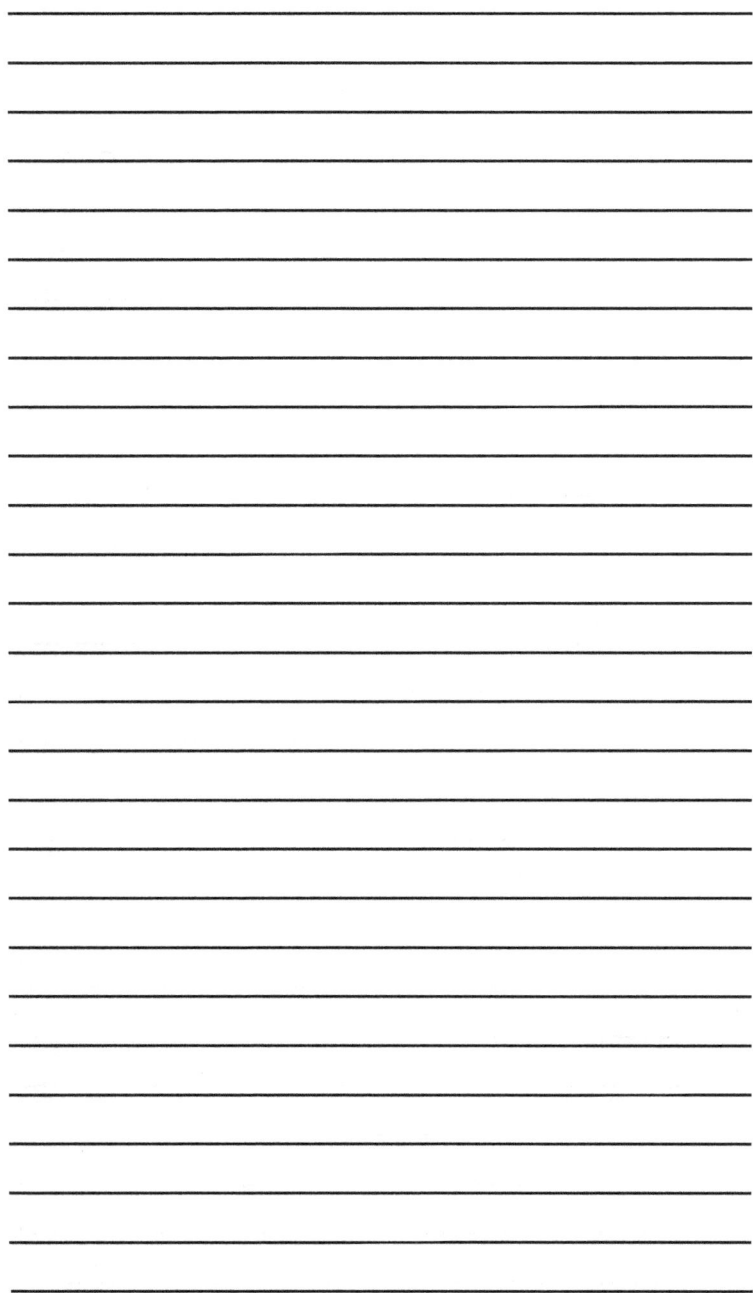

# ♠ Day Forty

_____

_____

_____

_____

_____

_____

_____

_____

_____

_____

_____

_____

_____

_____

_____

_____

_____

_____

_____

_____

_____

_____

# ♠ *Day Forty~One*

# ♠ *Day Forty~Two*

# ♠ *Day Forty~Three*

# ♠ *Day Forty~Four*

# ♠ Day Forty~Five

# ♠ *Day Forty~Six*

# ♠ *Day Forty~Seven*

# ♠ *Day Forty~Eight*

# ♠ Day Forty~Nine

# ♠ *Day Fifty*

# ♠ Day Fifty~One

# ♠ *Day Fifty~Two*

# ♠ *Day Fifty~Three*

# ♠ *Day Fifty~Four*

# ♠ Day Fifty~Five

# ♠ Day Fifty~Six

# ♠ *Day Fifty~Seven*

# ♠ Day Fifty~Eight

# ♠ Day Fifty~Nine

# ♠ *Day Sixty*

# ♠ *Day Sixty~One*

# ♠ *Day Sixty~Two*

# ♠ *Day Sixty~Three*

# ♠ *Day Sixty~Four*

# ♠ Day Sixty~Five

# ♠ *Day Sixty~Six*

# ♠ *Day Sixty~Seven*

# ♠ Day Sixty~Eight

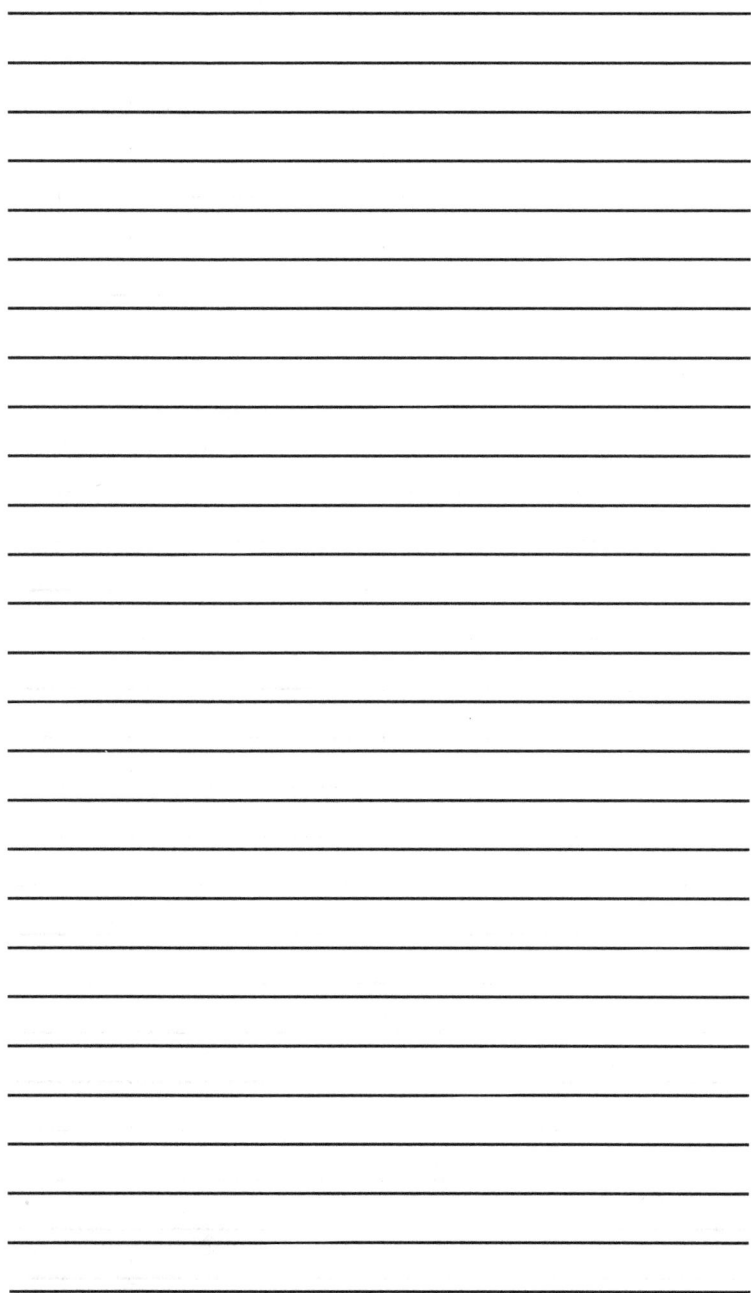

# ♠ *Day Sixty~Nine*

_____
_____
_____
_____
_____
_____
_____
_____
_____
_____
_____
_____
_____
_____
_____
_____
_____
_____
_____
_____
_____
_____
_____

# ♠ Day Seventy

# ♠ *Day Seventy~One*

# ♠ Day Seventy~Two

# ♠ *Day Seventy~Three*

# ♠ Day Seventy~Four

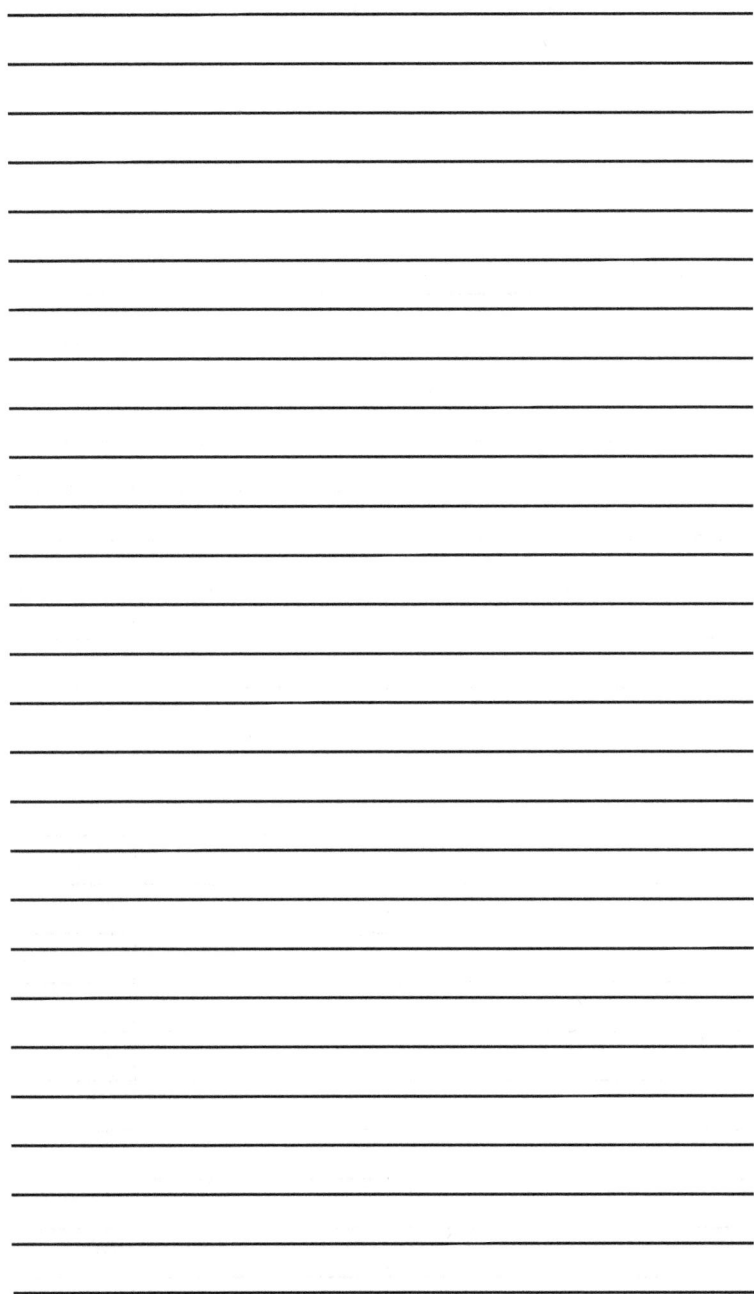

## ♠ *Day Seventy~Five*

_____

_____

_____

_____

_____

_____

_____

_____

_____

_____

_____

_____

_____

_____

_____

_____

_____

_____

_____

_____

_____

_____

# ♠ *Day Seventy~Six*

# ♠ *Day Seventy~Seven*

# ♠ *Day Seventy~Eight*

# ♠ Day Seventy~Nine

# ♠ *Day Eighty*

# ♠ *Day Eighty~One*

# ♠ *Day Eighty~Two*

# ♠ *Day Eighty~Three*

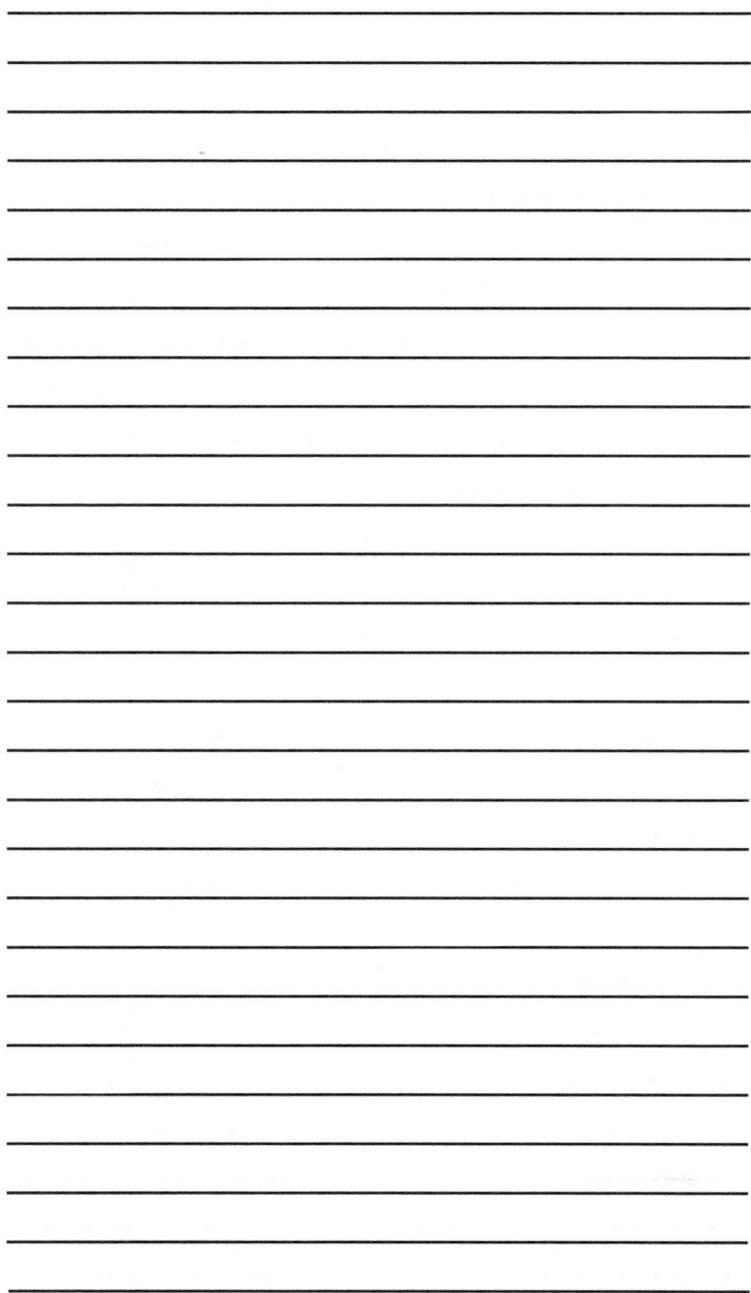

# ♠ *Day Eighty~Four*

_____

_____

_____

_____

_____

_____

_____

_____

_____

_____

_____

_____

_____

_____

_____

_____

_____

_____

_____

_____

_____

_____

_____

# ♠ *Day Eighty~Five*

# ♠ *Day Eighty~Six*

# ♠ *Day Eighty~Seven*

# ♠ *Day Eighty~Eight*

# ♠ Day Eighty~Nine

# ♠ *Day Ninety*

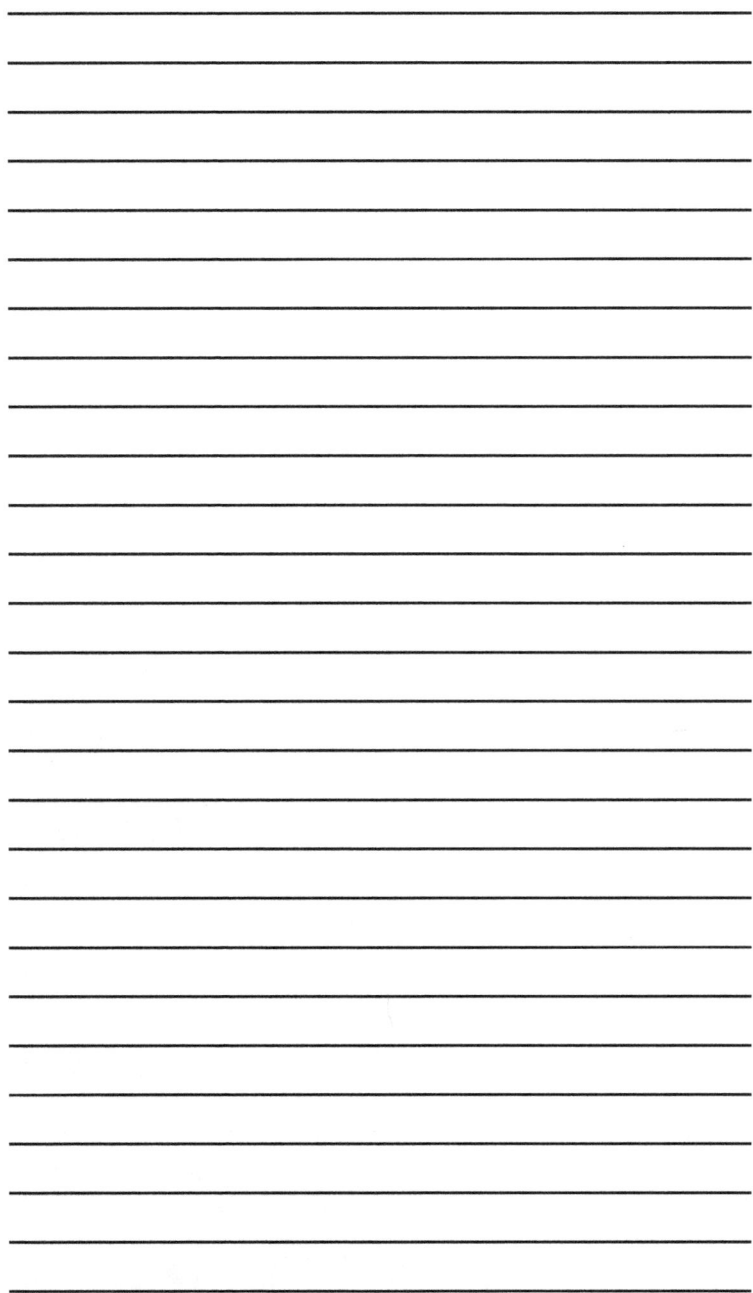

*Dear Sister,*

*I hope you can now take some time and read over your earlier days, and see how the Lord has been working in your life.*

*Don't stop hear. I urge you to continue with writing your daily prayers. Speaking to our Lord daily is something He desires more than anything.*

*Please remember that the Lord will ALWAYS be there for you and that he is a God of Love and Forgiveness!*

*I am so proud of you for going on this 90 day prayer journey,*

*Becky Brooks*

www.ingramcontent.com/pod-product-compliance
Lightning Source LLC
Chambersburg PA
CBHW060924040426
42445CB00011B/776